MY BAKING
Journal

spruce

An Hachette UK Company
www.hachette.co.uk

First published in Great Britain in 2012 by Spruce
a division of Octopus Publishing Group Ltd
Endeavour House
189 Shaftesbury Avenue
London
WC2H 8JY
www.octopusbooks.co.uk
www.octopusbooksusa.com

Distributed in the US by
Hachette Book Group USA
237 Park Avenue
New York NY 10017 USA

Distributed in Canada by
Canadian Manda Group
165 Dufferin Street
Toronto, Ontario, Canada M6K 3H6

ISBN 978-1-84601-394-2

A CIP catalogue record for this book is available from
the British Library.

Printed and bound in China

10 9 8 7 6 5 4 3 2 1

Publisher's note

Ovens should be preheated to the specific temperature.
If using a fan-assisted oven, follow the manufacturer's
instructions for adjusting the time and temperature.
Broilers should also be preheated.

This book includes dishes made with nuts and nut
derivatives. It is advisable for those with known allergic
reactions to nuts and nut derivatives and those who may
be potentially vulnerable to these allergies, such as
pregnant and nursing mothers, invalids, the elderly,
babies, and children, to avoid dishes make with nuts
and nut oils. It is also prudent to check the labels of
premade ingredients for the possible inclusion of nut
derivatives.

The US Department of Agriculture and the UK
Department of Health advise that eggs should not be
consumed raw unless they are pasteurized. This book
contains some dishes made with raw or lightly cooked
eggs. It is prudent for more vulnerable people, such as
pregnant and nursing mothers, invalids, the elderly,
babies, and young children, to avoid uncooked or lightly
cooked dishes made with eggs. If pasteurized eggs are
not available dried egg whites can be used instead.

Notes on the recipes

- Use US very large or British and Australian
large eggs
- Do not mix imperial and metric measurements
- 1 teaspoon = 5 ml
- 1 tablespoon = 15 ml
- 1 cup = 240 ml

Contents

Introduction 4
Baking Techniques & Know-How 6
Charts & Conversions 10
Glossary 11

Breads 12
Quick White Loaf 14
Mixed Seed Bread 15
Fruit Teacakes 16
Chocolate Brioche Loaf 17
Jottings & Tasting Notes 18
Journal Pages 20

Pastries & Pies 40
Rich Shortcrust Pastry 42
Sweet Shortcrust Pastry 42
Flaky Pastry 43
Quiche Lorraine 44
Beef, Oyster, & Ale Pie 45
Pumpkin Pie 46
Deep-Dish Apple Pie 47
Jottings & Tasting Notes 48
Journal Pages 50

Cakes & Muffins 70
Vanilla Cupcakes 72
Butterfly Cupcakes 72
Chocolate Cupcakes 72
Buttercreams—Plain, Vanilla, Citrus,
   Coffee, & Chocolate 73
Victoria Sandwich Sponge 74
Carrot & Walnut Cake 75
Cranberry Muffins 76
"English" Scones with Strawberry
   Preserve & Cream 77
Chocolate Party Cake 78
Rich Fruit Cake 80
Iced Fruit Cake 81

Marzipan 82
Royal Icing 83
Jottings & Tasting Notes 84
Journal Pages 86

Cookies & Traybakes 106
Chocolate Chip Cookies 108
Oatmeal & Raisin Cookies 108
Flapjacks 109
Linzer Cookies 110
Chewy Nut Chocolate Brownies 112
Chocolate Macaroons 113
Plain Almond Macaroons 113
White Chocolate & Pistachio Macaroons 113
Plain Cookie Dough 114
Glacé Icing & Decorating Cookies 114
Jottings & Tasting Notes 116
Journal pages 118

Desserts 138
Sticky Toffee Pudding 140
Rich Vanilla Custard 141
Chocolate Custard 141
Coffee Custard 141
Bread & Butter Pudding with Pecans 142
Vanilla Bean Crème Brûlée 143
Lemon Meringue Pie 144
Citrus Meringue Pie 145
Florentine Vanilla Cheesecake 146
Berry Crisp 147
Mini Pavlovas with Mixed Fresh Berries 148
Meringue Cookies 148
Hazelnut Meringues 149
Jottings & Tasting Notes 150
Journal Pages 152
Cook Again Recipe Notes 162

Acknowledgments 176

Introduction

Cooking and eating with friends and family is the greatest pastime there is, and your baking journal is the perfect place to store the recipes and memories that accompany these special occasions. Whether it's a recipe from one of your favorite cookbooks that you want to keep safe, a family heirloom, or a recipe shared between friends, you can now create your own ultimate baking cookbook by keeping a personalized baking journal to record all the wonderful memories you associate with food, baking, and time spent in your kitchen.

With a chapter dedicated to the different types of baking—breads, pastries and pies, cakes and muffins, cookies and traybakes, and desserts—there is a home for all those recipes you want to keep safe and never forget. Within each chapter you will find ample space to write out your recipes, along with baking and tasting notes and other pieces of information you want to remember. And at the end of the book there is a dedicated place to jot down the recipes you like to bake from other cookbooks and magazines, so never again will you forget where to find them.

We want your baking journal to be the most leafed-through cookbook and treasured possession in your kitchen, so you will also find more than 40 foolproof, classic recipes dotted throughout your journal—dishes no home-baker should be without—and an invaluable introductory section dedicated to useful baking technical know-how, handy hints, every conversion chart you will ever need, and a glossary for when you come across ingredient names you're not familiar with.

Baking Techniques & Know-How

Ingredients

Whatever the ingredient called for, it is important to use accurate amounts and measure correctly. The balance of ingredients, whether they are fats, flours, rising agents, or flavorings, are carefully calculated for each recipe, so it is important to follow the recommendations given. When baking, unless otherwise instructed, make sure that all ingredients are at room temperature. And one final thing before you start baking, you should always read the recipe through to ensure you have all the ingredients.

Successful Bread Making

🍞 Liquids should be warmed until they are tepid to help activate yeast.

🍞 If dough feels dry when it is first mixed, add more water a tablespoon at a time; if it feels very wet add more flour a tablespoon at a time.

🍞 Dough should be let rise in a draft-free place.

🍞 Lightly dust the work surface with flour when kneading or rolling dough.

🍞 Use a sharp knife to score dough and cut down without tearing.

🍞 To test if yeast bread is cooked tap gently underneath—it should sound hollow. If not, continue cooking for five minutes and retest.

🍞 Always transfer baked bread to a cooling rack to cool.

Successful Pastry Making

🍞 Use chilled butter from the refrigerator and make sure that water is cold or chilled.

🍞 Sift flours before using to help aerate the dough.

🍞 Add liquid to flour gradually so that you can stop before the dough feels too wet. You can add extra water, a little at a time, if the mixture feels too dry.

🍞 Work the dough as lightly and as quickly as possible, keeping it as cool as you can.

🍞 Knead and roll out dough on a lightly floured surface. If the dough is very soft or sticky, roll it out between pieces of parchment paper.

🍞 Roll dough in one direction from the center outwards, rotating it each time.

🍞 Never pull or stretch the dough as you roll it, as it will shrink back during cooking.

Successful Cake Making

🍴 Always follow the method and incorporate the ingredients in the order they are presented.

🍴 Eggs should be removed from the refrigerator 45 minutes before use.

🍴 When beating egg whites, make sure both the bowl and the beaters are clean and dry, otherwise they will not aerate properly.

🍴 Add eggs to a creamed mixture gradually, beating well after each addition. If the mixture starts to curdle, beat in a little of the flour after each egg.

🍴 Sift the flour and rising agent together so they are evenly dispersed.

🍴 When you fold in dry ingredients, work gently from the center of the bowl outwards, turning the bowl a little with each fold.

🍴 Always level the surface of the batter in the pan before baking. For cakes that take more than one hour to cook, make a shallow indentation in the center of the batter to allow for even rising.

🍴 Never open the oven door during the first half of the cooking time.

🍴 To test if a cake is cooked, insert a metal skewer in the center, wait three seconds, and remove. It should be clean and dry. If not, return the cake to the oven and test again after five minutes. Lighter-textured cakes should have shrunk slightly away from the side of the pan.

Successful Cookie Making

🍴 Chilled butter should be used straight from the refrigerator. Softened butter should be removed at least 1 hour before use.

🍴 Eggs should be removed from the refrigerator at least 45 minutes before use.

🍴 Make sure the oven shelves are set an equal distance apart if you are cooking more than one cookie sheet at a time.

🍴 Because some cookies spread during cooking, always leave a gap between them to be safe.

🍴 Never put cookie dough on hot cookie sheets.

🍴 Always cook cookies for the minimum time given. If they are not cooked, return to the oven and check them every minute—they can brown very quickly.

🍴 Cool cookies on a cooling rack, unless otherwise indicated, and allow cookies to cool completely before decorating or filling.

Mixing Techniques

MELTING METHOD Melt the fat and sugar in a saucepan with other liquid ingredients, but not the eggs, and keep the heat low to dissolve the ingredients without boiling. Remove from the heat and cool slightly before stirring in the eggs, followed quickly by the flour and spices until evenly combined. The heat starts to activate the rising agent straight away, so the quicker you put the mixture in the oven, the better it will rise.

BEATING & WHISKING Use a wooden spoon or handheld electric mixer when ingredients need to be combined briskly while still incorporating plenty of air, such as making muffins. To whisk, use a large balloon whisk and beat the batter quickly, lifting the whisk from the bowl and combining the ingredients in a fast, circular motion to incorporate a maximum amount of air. Plenty of electric mixers will do this for you.

FOLDING A technique used when ingredients need to be combined gently, while incorporating as much air into the mixture as possible. Use a large, metal spoon that will slice through the mixture easily. Touching the bottom of the bowl with the spoon, adopt a cutting motion through the center of the mixture, folding over when you reach the side of the bowl to unearth the pockets of flour and other dry ingredients.

RUBBING IN This technique is normally used to rub butter into flour, and is easiest if the butter is cold and has been diced first. Rub the pieces of butter into the flour in a large bowl using the fingertips and lifting the mixture at the same time, letting it fall back into the bowl. The lifting stops the ingredients from clumping together and gives a texture of fine bread crumbs.

Greasing & Lining a Pan

ROUND PANS Position the base of the pan on parchment paper, draw around the perimeter, and then cut out the circle. Next, cut strips of paper about 1 inch (2.5 cm) wider than the height of the pan, fold over a ½-inch (1-cm) lip and snip it at intervals. Lightly grease the pan, then fit the paper around the sides so the lip sits flat on the base. If you need more than one strip of paper to go round the sides, overlap them slightly. Press the circle onto the base over the lip.

RECTANGULAR AND SQUARE PANS This technique is similar to the one above, but once you've cut the base and strips, you only need to make snips in the paper at the corners to make sure it fits squarely into the corners of the pan.

Storing Baked Goods

🍴 BREAD that is home-baked can be stored for up to 24 hours in a paper or cloth bag in a cool place, but not the refrigerator. To freeze bread, wrap it in plastic wrap and then put this in a freezer bag. Defrost to room temperature and slice as normal.

🍴 CAKES can be stored wrapped loosely in foil and kept in an airtight container in a cool place for two or three days; heavy fruit cakes will keep longer. Sponge and butter cakes can be frozen before they are filled or iced, wrapped in plastic wrap. Defrost at room temperature before icing.

🍴 PASTRIES are best stored in airtight containers, and if they are filled with cream stored in the refrigerator. Pastry can be frozen raw in a block or as a raw shell, covered in plastic wrap. Blind-baked crusts can be frozen in a freezer bag ready for filling.

🍴 COOKIES keep really well, especially the plainer types. Store them in plastic containers or airtight jars. Slices keep well too and should be stored in airtight containers.

Charts & Conversions

The recipes in this journal list both imperial and metric measures, however, when you are cooking from other recipes it may not always be this simple. Because we want your journal to be your most treasured possession in the kitchen, we have included here charts of all the measurements and pan sizes you are likely to need. There is also a conversion table for butter so baking recipes from around the world is that much simpler. A word of warning, to ensure the best result, never mix your measures—choose either imperial and cups or metric—and stay with the same system. Cup measures are based on the American imperial measuring cup. One American cup holds 8 fl oz, 16 tablespoons, or 240 ml.

Liquid

AMERICAN	IMPERIAL	METRIC
1 teaspoon	1 teaspoon	5 ml
1 tablespoon	½ fl oz	15 ml
2 tablespoons	1 fl oz	30 ml
¼ cup	2 fl oz	60 ml
⅓ cup	2¾ fl oz	85 ml
½ cup	4 fl oz	120 ml
¾ cup	6 fl oz	180 ml
1 cup	8 fl oz	240 ml
1¼ cups	10 fl oz	300 ml
2½ cups	20 fl oz	600 ml
4½ cups	34 fl oz	1 liter

🥄 1 American pint is 450 ml whereas the British pint is 600 ml

🥄 1 Australian tablespoon is equivalent to 15 ml

Weight

IMPERIAL	METRIC
¼ oz	10 g
½ oz	15 g
¾ oz	20 g
1 oz	25 g
4 oz	115 g
4½ oz	125 g
6 oz	175 g
7 oz	200 g
8 oz	225 g
12 oz	340 g
1 lb	450 g

Dimensions

IMPERIAL	METRIC
1 inch	2.5 cm
2 inches	5 cm
3¼ inches	8 cm
3½ inches	9 cm
4 inches	10 cm
5 inches	12.5 cm
7 inches	18 cm
8 inches	20 cm
9 inches	23 cm
10 inches	25.5 cm
11 inches	27.5 cm
11¼ inches	28 cm
12 inches	30 cm

Glossary

AMERICAN TERM	BRITISH TERM
allspice	*mixed spice*
almonds, slivered	*almonds, flaked*
bacon, Canadian	*smoked back bacon*
broiler, to broil	*grill, to grill*
cake pan	*cake tin*
cherries, candied	*cherries, glacé*
chocolate, semisweet or bittersweet	
	chocolate, plain dark
cornstarch	*cornflour*
crackers, graham	*biscuits, digestive*
cream, heavy	*cream, double*
cream, light	*cream, single*
Dutch oven	*cast-iron casserole*
flour, all-purpose	*flour, plain*
flour, bread	*flour, strong white*
flour, self-rising	*flour, self-raising*
instant espresso powder	*coffee granules*
liners, paper	*cups, paper*
molasses, dark	*black treacle*
paper, parchment	*paper, baking*
paper towel	*kitchen towel*
premade	*ready-made*
preserve	*jam*
raisins, golden	*sultanas*
skillet	*frying pan*
sugar, confectioners'	*sugar, icing*
sugar, dark brown	*sugar, dark muscovado*
sugar, light brown	*sugar, light muscovado*
sugar, superfine	*sugar, caster*
syrup, corn	*golden syrup*
vanilla bean	*vanilla pod*
vegetable shortening	*white vegetable fat*
wrap, plastic	*clingfilm*
yeast, active dry	*yeast, fast-action dried*
yogurt, plain	*yogurt, natural*

Oven temperatures

°FAHRENHEIT	°CELSIUS	GAS MARK
225°F	110°C	¼
250°F	120°C	½
275°F	135°C	2
300°F	150°C	2
325°F	160°C	3
350°F	180°C	4
375°F	190°C	5
400°F	200°C	6
425°F	220°C	7
450°F	230°C	8

Butter conversions

AMERICAN STICK	METRIC
1 tablespoon	15 g
2 tablespoons (¼ stick)	25 g
3 tablespoons	40 g
4 tablespoons (½ stick)	60 g
5 tablespoons	75 g
6 tablespoons (¾ stick)	85 g
7 tablespoons	100 g
8 tablespoons (1 stick)	115 g

BREADS

"No dinner without bread."

Russian proverb

Quick White Loaf

Preparation time 20 minutes,
  plus rising
Cooking time 25–30 minutes
Makes 1 loaf

Small 1 lb 1 oz (500 g)
2⅔ cups (11 oz/325 g) bread flour,
  plus extra for dusting
1 tablespoon milk powder
2 teaspoons superfine sugar
½ teaspoon salt
1¾ teaspoons active dry yeast
1 tablespoon sunflower oil, plus
  extra for greasing
scant 1 cup (7 fl oz/200 ml)
  warm water

Large 1 lb 10 oz (750 g)
4 cups (1 lb 1 oz/500 g) bread flour,
  plus extra for dusting
2 tablespoons milk powder
1 tablespoon superfine sugar
1 teaspoon salt
2½ teaspoons active dry yeast
2 tablespoons sunflower oil, plus
  extra for greasing
1¼ cups (10 fl oz/300 ml)
  warm water

🍃 Mix the flour, milk powder, sugar, salt, and yeast in a large bowl. Add the oil and gradually mix in enough warm water to make a soft dough.

🍃 Knead well on a lightly floured surface for 10 minutes until the dough is smooth and elastic. Put in a loaf pan, depending on the size of the dough. Cover loosely with oiled plastic wrap and let rise in a warm place 45 minutes or until the dough reaches just above the top of the pan.

🍃 Remove the plastic wrap and bake in a preheated oven, 400°F (200°C, Gas Mark 6), 25 minutes for the small loaf or 30 minutes for the large loaf, or until the bread is golden and sounds hollow when tapped on the base. Check larger loaves after 15 minutes and cover with foil if overbrowning. Holding the pan with oven mitts, loosen the bread with a metal spatula. Transfer to a cooling rack to cool.

Mixed Seed Bread

Preparation time 25 minutes,
  plus rising
Cooking time 30–35 minutes
Makes 1 large loaf

4⅓ cups (1 lb ½ oz/475 g) malted
  barley flour, plus extra for
  dusting
2 tablespoons (1 oz/25 g) butter
1 tablespoon light brown sugar
1½ teaspoons salt
3 tablespoons sesame seeds
3 tablespoons sunflower seeds

3 tablespoons flaxseeds
1¼ teaspoons active dry yeast
1¼ cups (10 fl oz/300 ml) warm water
vegetable oil, for greasing

To finish
milk, to glaze
extra seeds, optional

🍞 Put the flour into a large bowl, add the butter, and rub in with the fingertips until the mixture resembles fine bread crumbs. Stir in the sugar, salt, seeds, and yeast. Gradually mix in enough warm water to make a soft dough. Turn out onto a lightly floured surface and knead for 5 minutes or until the dough is smooth and elastic. Put back into the bowl, cover loosely with oiled plastic wrap, and let rise in a warm place 1 hour or until doubled.

🍞 Turn the dough out onto a lightly floured surface and knead 5 minutes more. Put the dough into a greased 8-inch (20-cm) round loose-bottomed pan. Cover loosely with oiled plastic wrap and let rise in a warm place 30 minutes or until the dough reaches the top of the pan.

🍞 Brush with milk to glaze, sprinkle with extra seeds, if using, and bake in a preheated oven, 400°F (200°C, Gas Mark 6), 30–35 minutes until the bread is golden and sounds hollow when tapped on the base. Cover with foil after 15 minutes to prevent overbrowning. Holding the pan with oven mitts, loosen the bread with a metal spatula. Transfer to a cooling rack to cool.

Fruit Teacakes

Preparation time 30 minutes,
    plus rising
Cooking time 15–20 minutes
Makes 8

3²⁄₃ cups (1 lb/450 g) bread flour, sifted,
    plus extra for dusting
1¼ teaspoons active dry yeast
½ teaspoon salt
1 teaspoon ground allspice
scant 1 cup (5¼ oz/150 g) mixed dried fruit
⅓ cup (2¾ oz/75 g) light brown sugar
2 teaspoons vanilla bean paste or vanilla extract
1¼ cups (10 fl oz/300 ml) milk
3½ tablespoons (1¾ oz/50 g) unsalted butter, melted

To finish
1 egg, beaten, to glaze
superfine sugar, for sprinkling

&. Combine the flour, yeast, salt, allspice, mixed dried fruit, and sugar in the bowl of an electric mixer. Add the vanilla bean paste, milk, and melted butter. Set the mixer to low and work the ingredients together to form a soft dough. Increase the speed to high and knead for 8–10 minutes until the dough is smooth and elastic. Place the dough in an oiled bowl, cover with a dish towel, and let rise in a warm place 1 hour or until doubled.

&. Knock back the dough on a lightly floured surface. Divide into 8 equal-sized pieces and shape each into a small bun. Press the buns into a lightly oiled 12 x 8-inch (30 x 20-cm) cake pan, cover with oiled plastic wrap, and let rise for 30 minutes more or until the dough doubles. Brush with beaten egg to glaze and bake in a preheated oven, 425°F (220°C, Gas Mark 7), 15–20 minutes until risen and golden. Transfer to a cooling rack to cool and sprinkle with superfine sugar.

Chocolate Brioche Loaf

Preparation time 25 minutes,
   plus rising
Cooking time 30 minutes
Makes 8–10 slices

2 cups (9 oz/250 g) bread flour,
   plus extra for dusting
pinch of salt
scant ¼ cup (1¾ oz/50 g) superfine sugar
2 teaspoons active dry yeast
3½ tablespoons (1¾ oz/50 g) unsalted
   butter, plus extra for greasing
2 eggs, beaten
3 tablespoons (1¾ fl oz/50 ml) milk, warmed
1¾ oz (50 g) semisweet chocolate chips
1 egg, to glaze

❧ Mix together the flour, salt, sugar, and yeast. Heat the butter in a small saucepan until it has melted but don't let it boil. Set aside to cool a little. Grease a 10-flute (5-cup/40-fl-oz/1.20-liter) brioche mold.

❧ Mix the eggs and milk together. Pour into the flour followed by the cooled butter. Bring the mixture together to form a soft dough and knead by hand for 10 minutes or with a dough hook in a mixer for 5 minutes. Turn into a lightly oiled bowl, cover with oiled plastic wrap, and let rise in a warm place for about 1 hour or until doubled. Turn the dough out onto a floured surface and knock out the air. Knead in the chocolate chips, shape into a round, and place in the greased mold. Let rise in a warm place 15 minutes.

❧ Beat the egg with 1 tablespoon water, then brush the surface with some of the egg glaze. Bake in a preheated oven, 400°F (200°C, Gas Mark 6), 15 minutes. Turn the heat down to 350°F (180°C, Gas Mark 4) and continue to cook for 15 minutes more. Let cool in the mold for 5 minutes, then turn out onto a cooling rack to cool completely.

Jottings & Tasting Notes

Use these pages to keep track of your favorite recipes from cookbooks, food magazines, and even websites. Simply fill in the recipe name along with the source, for example, the name of the cookbook and the relevant page number, plus any other notes you'd like to make.

Recipe

Source

Baking Notes

Recipe

Source

Baking Notes

Recipe

Source

Baking Notes

Recipe

Source

Baking Notes

Recipe

Source

Baking Notes

Recipe

Source

Baking Notes

Recipe

Source

Baking Notes

Recipe

Source

Baking Notes

Recipe

Source

Baking Notes

Recipe

Source

Makes/Serves

Testing & Tasting Notes

Ingredients

Method

Recipe

Source

Makes/Serves

Testing & Tasting Notes

Ingredients

Method

Recipe

Source

Makes/Serves

Testing & Tasting Notes

Ingredients

Method

"Part of the secret in life is to eat what you like and let the food fight it out inside."

Mark Twain

Recipe

Source

Makes/Serves

Testing & Tasting Notes

Ingredients

Method

Recipe

Source

Makes/Serves

Testing & Tasting Notes

Ingredients

Method

Recipe
Source
Makes/Serves
Testing & Tasting Notes

Ingredients

Method

"So long as you have food in your mouth, you have solved all the questions for the time being."

Franz Kafka

Recipe

Source

Makes/Serves

Testing & Tasting Notes

Ingredients

Method

Recipe

Source

Makes/Serves

Testing & Tasting Notes

Ingredients

Method

"A good meal ought to begin with hunger."

French proverb

Recipe
Source
Makes/Serves
Testing & Tasting Notes

Ingredients

Method

Recipe

Source

Makes/Serves

Testing & Tasting Notes

Ingredients

Method

"All sorrows are less with bread."

Miguel de Cervantes,
Don Quixote

PASTRIES
& PIES

"The proof of the pudding is in the eating."

English proverb

Rich Shortcrust Pastry

Preparation time 10–15 minutes,
   plus chilling
Makes 13¼ oz (375 g),
   enough for one 10-inch
   (25-cm) pie pan

scant 1⅔ cups (7 oz/200 g) all-purpose flour,
   sifted, plus extra for dusting
½ teaspoon salt
1⅛ sticks (4½ oz/125 g) butter, chilled
   and diced
1 egg yolk
2–3 tablespoons cold water

❧ Put the flour and salt in a food processor or electric blender, add the butter, and pulse briefly until the mixture resembles fine bread crumbs. Add the egg yolk and water, a tablespoon at a time, and process again until the pastry just starts to come together. Transfer the dough to a lightly floured surface, knead gently, and form into a flat disc. Cover with plastic wrap and chill 30 minutes. Remove from the refrigerator and roll the dough out on a lightly floured surface according to the recipe.

Variation

❧ For Sweet Shortcrust Pastry, process as above 2 cups (9 oz/250 g) all-purpose flour, sifted, 2 tablespoons confectioners' sugar, 1⅛ sticks (4½ oz/125 g) diced unsalted butter, and 4½ oz (125 g) diced vegetable shortening (or you can use all butter) until the mixture resembles fine bread crumbs. Add 8 teaspoons cold water and process again until the pastry just starts to come together. Knead on a lightly floured surface, form into a flat disc, cover in plastic wrap, and chill 15 minutes. Continue according to the recipe. This recipe makes 1 lb (450 g) pastry, enough to fill a 12-inch (30-cm) tart pan.

Flaky Pastry

**Preparation time 15–20 minutes,
    plus chilling
Makes 1 lb 1 oz (500 g) pastry
    or enough to top a 9-inch
    (23-cm) deep-dish pie pan**

2 cups (9 oz/250 g) all-purpose flour, sifted,
    plus extra for dusting
pinch of salt
2¾ oz (75 g) vegetable shortening
    or lard, chilled and diced
5 tablespoons (2¾ oz/75 g) unsalted butter,
    chilled and diced
2 teaspoons lemon juice
5–6 tablespoons cold water

❧ Place the flour and salt in a bowl, add one-quarter of the vegetable shortening and one-quarter of the butter, and rub in with the fingertips until the mixture resembles fine bread crumbs. Add the lemon juice, mixing with a metal spatula, then enough cold water to form a soft but not sticky dough. Knead lightly on a lightly floured surface, then roll out to form a rough rectangle, about 18 x 6 inches (45 x 15 cm).

❧ Dot half the remaining shortening and butter over the bottom two-thirds of the pastry. Fold over the top one-third of the dough and then fold up the bottom third to enclose the fat. Press the edges together to seal, then give the dough a quarter turn. Roll out the pastry again, dot with the remaining fats and fold, as before. Give a quarter turn, then roll and fold twice more. Cover in plastic wrap and chill 30 minutes before using according to the recipe.

Quiche Lorraine

Preparation time 20 minutes,
    plus chilling time
Cooking time 55–60 minutes
Serves 4–6

Pastry

scant 1½ cups (6 oz/175 g)
    all-purpose flour, sifted
5 tablespoons (2¾ oz/75 g) butter,
    chilled and diced
1 egg yolk, beaten

Filling

6 oz (175 g) rindless Canadian bacon
generous 1 cup (8½ fl oz/250 ml)
    light cream
2 eggs, beaten
grated nutmeg
sea salt and freshly ground pepper

❧ Place the flour in a bowl. Add the butter and mix together with your fingertips until the mixture resembles fine bread crumbs. Add the egg yolk and enough cold water, about 1–2 tablespoons, to mix to a firm dough. Cover with plastic wrap and chill 30 minutes.

❧ Roll out the dough on a lightly floured surface and use to line a 9-inch (23-cm) pie pan. Chill the pastry shell 30 minutes. Meanwhile preheat the oven to 400°F (200°C, Gas Mark 6). Fill the pastry shell with crumpled foil and bake in the preheated oven 15 minutes. Remove the foil, lower the oven temperature to 350°F (180°C, Gas Mark4), and bake 10 minutes more.

❧ Meanwhile make the filling. Broil the bacon until crisp, then drain on paper towel and crumble or cut into pieces. Beat the cream, eggs, and nutmeg in a bowl and season with salt and pepper. Sprinkle the bacon in the blind-baked crust and pour the cream and egg filling over the top. Place on a cookie sheet in the preheated oven and bake 30–35 minutes until the filling is just set and the pastry golden. Serve the quiche warm or cold.

Beef, Oyster, & Ale Pie

Preparation time 1 hour
Cooking time 2–2½ hours
Serves 4

2 lb 4 oz (1 kg) stewing steak, cubed
1 tablespoon all-purpose flour
2 tablespoons (1 oz/25 g) butter
1 onion, chopped
1 garlic clove, crushed
2 carrots, chopped
2 celery ribs, chopped
1 tablespoon chopped thyme
2 tablespoons olive oil

2½ cups (20 fl oz/600 ml) stout
14 oz (400 g) canned diced
    tomatoes
2 bay leaves
12 large oysters, shucked
12¼ oz (350 g) premade puff pastry
    or flaky pastry (see page 43)
1 egg, beaten
sea salt and freshly ground pepper

🍃 Put the steak in a bowl. Add the flour, season with salt and pepper, and mix until the meat is coated in flour. Melt the butter in a heavy-based Dutch oven and fry the onion, garlic, carrots, celery, and thyme until the vegetables are soft. Remove with a slotted spoon, then add the oil to the pot and fry the beef until browned. Stir in the vegetables, add the stout, and scrape any sticky bits off the base of the pan. Add the tomatoes and bay leaves, bring to a boil, cover, and simmer 1–1½ hours until the beef is tender. Discard the bay leaves and stir in the oysters and any juices.

🍃 Preheat the oven to 400°F (200°C, Gas Mark 6) and oil a 9-inch (23-cm) deep-dish pie pan. Roll out the pastry on a lightly floured surface to ⅛ inch (2 mm) thick and about 1 inch (2.5 cm) larger than the pan. Tip the stew into the pan and brush the rim with a little beaten egg.

🍃 Lay the pastry over the top, pressing down well, and trim the edge. Press your first and second fingers along the pie edge to create a fluted pattern, then score between the scallops with a sharp knife. Cut out leaf shapes from the pastry trimmings. Brush the pastry lid with beaten egg and press the leaves into the center to form a pattern. Pierce a small slit in the middle, brush again with the egg, and bake in the preheated oven 35–40 minutes until the pastry is risen and golden.

Pumpkin Pie

Preparation time 30 minutes
Cooking time 1–1¼ hours
Serves 6

1 lb (450 g) pumpkin or butternut
squash, weighed after seeding
and peeling, diced
3 eggs
½ cup (3½ oz/100 g) light brown
sugar
2 tablespoons all-purpose flour, plus
extra for dusting
½ teaspoon ground cinnamon

½ teaspoon ground ginger
¼ teaspoon grated nutmeg
scant 1 cup (7 fl oz/200 ml) milk,
plus extra for glazing
1 lb (450 g) premade or sweet
shortcrust pastry (see page 42),
chilled
confectioners' sugar, for dusting
whipped cream, to serve

Steam the pumpkin 15–20 minutes until tender. Cool, then puree in a blender or food processor.

Beat the eggs, sugar, flour, and spices together in a bowl until just mixed. Beat in the pumpkin puree, then gradually mix in the milk. Set aside. Preheat the oven to 375°F (190°C, Gas Mark 5).

Roll out three-quarters of the pastry on a lightly floured surface until large enough to line a 9-inch (23-cm) pie pan. Line the pie pan with the pastry. Trim off the excess around the rim and add to the reserved pastry. Roll out the trimmings thinly and cut out leaves, then mark with veins. Brush the rim of the pastry in the dish with milk, then press on the leaves.

Place the pie plate on a cookie sheet and pour in the pumpkin filling. Then brush the dish edges lightly with milk. Bake in the preheated oven 45–55 minutes until the filling is set and the pastry cooked through. Cover with foil after 20 minutes to stop the pastry edge overbrowning. Dust the pie with confectioners' sugar before serving warm or cold with whipped cream.

Deep-Dish Apple Pie

Preparation time 40 minutes, plus chilling
Cooking time 20–25 minutes
Serves 6

2 lb 4 oz (1 kg) or about 5 cooking apples,
    quartered, cored, peeled, and thickly sliced
½ cup (3½ oz/100 g) superfine sugar, plus
    extra for sprinkling
grated zest of 1 small orange
½ teaspoon ground cinnamon
3 whole cloves
1 quantity shortcrust pastry (see page 42), chilled
a little flour, for dusting
1 egg, beaten
heavy cream, to serve

🍃 Fill a 9-inch (23-cm) deep-dish pie plate with the apples. Mix the sugar with the orange zest, cinnamon, and cloves, then sprinkle over the apples.

🍃 Preheat the oven to 400°F (200°C, Gas Mark 6). Roll the pastry out on a lightly floured surface until a little larger than the top of the pie plate. Cut 2 long strips from the edges, about ½ inch (1 cm) wide. Brush the plate rim with a little beaten egg, then press the strips on top. Lift the rolled pastry over the plate and line the plate, pressing the edges together.

🍃 Trim the excess with a sharp knife and press your first and second fingers along the pie edge to create a fluted pattern, then score between the scallops with a sharp knife. Reroll the trimmings and cut out small heart shapes or circles with a small cookie cutter. Brush the pastry lid with beaten egg and press the shapes into the center to form a pattern. Brush again with the egg, sprinkle over a little extra sugar, and bake in the preheated oven 20–25 minutes until the pastry is risen and golden. Serve warm with spoonfuls of heavy cream.

Jottings & Tasting Notes

Use these pages to keep track of your favorite recipes from cookbooks, food magazines, and even websites. Simply fill in the recipe name along with the source, for example, the name of the cookbook and the relevant page number, plus any other notes you'd like to make.

Recipe

Source

Baking Notes

Recipe

Source

Baking Notes

Recipe

Source

Baking Notes

Recipe

Source

Baking Notes

Recipe

Source
Baking Notes

Recipe

Source
Baking Notes

Recipe

Source
Baking Notes

Recipe

Source
Baking Notes

Recipe

Source
Baking Notes

Recipe

Source

Makes/Serves

Testing & Tasting Notes

Ingredients

Method

*"There is no love sincerer
than the love of food."*

George Bernard Shaw

Recipe

Source

Makes/Serves

Testing & Tasting Notes

Ingredients

Method

Recipe

Source

Makes/Serves

Testing & Tasting Notes

Ingredients

Method

Recipe

Source

Makes/Serves

Testing & Tasting Notes

Ingredients

Method

Recipe

Source

Makes/Serves

Testing & Tasting Notes

Ingredients

Method

"I feel a recipe is only a theme, which an intelligent cook can play each time with a variation."

Madame Benoit

Recipe

Source

Makes/Serves

Testing & Tasting Notes

Ingredients

Method

Recipe

Source

Makes/Serves

Testing & Tasting Notes

Ingredients

Method

Recipe

Source

Makes/Serves

Testing & Tasting Notes

Ingredients

Method

Recipe

Source

Makes/Serves

Testing & Tasting Notes

Ingredients

Method

> *"A good cook is like a sorceress who dispenses happiness."*
>
> Elsa Schiaparelli

Recipe
Source
Makes/Serves
Testing & Tasting Notes

Ingredients

Method

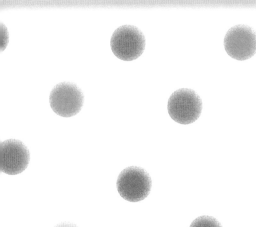

CAKES &
MUFFINS

*"Anything is good if it's
made of chocolate."*

Jo Brand

Vanilla Cupcakes

**Preparation time 10 minutes,
plus decorating
Cooking time 20 minutes
Makes 12**

1⅜ sticks (5½ oz/150 g) unsalted butter,
    softened
¾ cup (5½ oz/150 g) superfine sugar
1½ cups (6 oz/175 g) self-rising flour
3 eggs
1 teaspoon vanilla extract

&. Preheat the oven to 350°F (180°C, Gas Mark 4) and line a 12-cup standard muffin pan with paper cups. Put all the cake ingredients in a bowl and beat until light and creamy, then divide the batter into the paper cups—each should be approximately three-quarters full.

&. Place the cupcakes in the preheated oven and bake 20 minutes or until risen and just firm to the touch. Remove from the oven and cool in the pan on a cooling rack. Delicious served plain or topped with your favorite buttercream (see opposite).

Variations

&. To make Butterfly Cupcakes, you will need 1 quantity of buttercream (see opposite). Using a small, sharp knife neatly cut out a circle of sponge from the middle of each cooled cake, then cut each round in half. Fill the cavity of each cake with vanilla buttercream, then replace the tops so they resemble butterfly wings. If liked, you could place a dollop of strawberry preserve between the sponge wings.

&. For Chocolate Cupcakes, make the cake mixture as above, but substitute 1 tablespoon unsweetened cocoa powder for 1 tablespoon of the flour.

Buttercream

Preparation time 5 minutes
Makes enough to
cover 12 cupcakes

1⅜ sticks (5¼ oz/150 g) unsalted butter,
    softened
2 cups (9 oz/250 g) confectioners' sugar,
    sifted
2 teaspoons hot water

🍃 Beat the butter and a little of the confectioners' sugar together in a bowl until smooth. Gradually beat in the remaining confectioners' sugar and hot water until pale and creamy.

Variations

🍃 For Vanilla Buttercream add 1 teaspoon vanilla extract.

🍃 For Citrus Buttercream add 2–3 teaspoons finely grated lemon, lime, or orange zest and replace the hot water with fruit juice.

🍃 For Coffee Buttercream dissolve 2 teaspoons instant espresso powder in the hot water.

🍃 For Chocolate Buttercream mix 2 tablespoons each of hot water and unsweetened cocoa powder until smooth, then beat into the creamed butter and sugar.

Victoria Sandwich Sponge

Preparation time 20 minutes
Cooking time 25 minutes
Serves 8

1½ sticks (6 oz/175 g) unsalted butter,
    softened, plus extra for greasing
generous ¾ cup (6 oz/175 g) superfine sugar
3 eggs, beaten
1½ cups (6 oz/175 g) self-rising flour
5 tablespoons strawberry or
    raspberry preserve
confectioners' sugar, for dusting

❧ Preheat the oven to 350°F (180°C, Gas Mark 6) and grease and line the base and sides of two 7-inch (18-cm) round baking pans with parchment paper.

❧ Beat the butter and sugar in a large bowl until the ingredients are pale in color and fluffy. Add the eggs one at a time, beating well after each addition—make sure the mixture is thick and smooth before adding the next egg. If the mixture starts to curdle, beat in a spoonful of the flour.

❧ Sift the flour into the bowl then, using a large metal spoon, fold the flour into the egg mixture. Don't beat or over mix, or you will knock out all the air. Divide the batter between the two pans and level the surface. Place in the preheated oven and bake 25 minutes or until risen and just firm to the touch. Remove from the oven, loosen the edges of the sponge, and turn out onto a cooling rack. Peel off the parchment paper and let cool completely.

❧ When cold, sandwich the sponges with the preserve and sprinkle generously with confectioners' sugar.

Carrot & Walnut Cake

Preparation time 35 minutes
Cooking time 25 minutes
Serves 10

butter, for greasing
scant ⅔ cup (5 fl oz/150 ml)
    sunflower oil
3 eggs
generous ¾ cup (6 oz/175 g) light
    brown sugar
1½ cups (6 oz/175 g) self-rising flour
1½ teaspoons baking powder
grated zest of ½ orange
1 teaspoon ground cinnamon
1¼ cups (5¼ oz/150 g) carrots,
    coarsely grated

scant ½ cup (1¾ oz/50 g) walnuts,
    finely chopped
5 walnut halves, halved, to decorate

Cream cheese frosting

4 tablespoons (2 oz/60 g) butter,
    softened
5 ¾ oz (160 g) cream cheese,
    softened
2 teaspoons grated lemon zest
4 cups (1 lb/450 g) confectioners'
    sugar, sifted

⁂ Preheat the oven to 350°F (180°C, Gas Mark 4) and grease and line the base and sides of two 8-inch (20-cm) round baking pans with parchment paper.

⁂ Put the oil, eggs, and sugar in a bowl and beat together until smooth. Add the flour, baking powder, orange zest, and ground cinnamon and beat again until smooth. Stir in the grated carrots and chopped nuts. Divide the mixture into the baking pans, level the surface, and place in the preheated oven about 20 minutes or until the tops spring back when pressed. Cool 5 minutes in the pans, then turn out onto a cooling rack and peel off the parchment paper. Let cool completely.

⁂ To make the cream cheese frosting, beat the butter, cream cheese, and lemon zest in a small bowl with an electric mixer until light and fluffy. Gradually beat in the confectioners' sugar.

⁂ Sandwich the 2 cake layers together with frosting, then transfer to a serving plate. Swirl the remaining frosting over the top and sides of the cake and decorate with the walnut halves.

Cranberry Muffins

Preparation time 10 minutes
Cooking time 20 minutes
Makes 15

1 egg
scant ½ cup (3½ fl oz/100 ml) milk
5 tablespoons (2¾ oz/75 g) unsalted butter,
    softened, plus extra for greasing
1¼ cups (5¼ oz/150 g) all-purpose flour, sifted
3 teaspoons baking powder
½ cup (3½ oz/100 g) superfine sugar
scant ⅔ cup (2¾ oz/75 g) frozen cranberries,
    partially defrosted

Topping
2 tablespoons superfine or confectioners' sugar
1 teaspoon ground cinnamon

🥄 Preheat the oven to 350°F (180°C, Gas Mark 4) and grease 15 standard muffin cups (you will need two pans). Alternatively, line the cups with paper cups, if preferred.

🥄 Put the egg and milk in a bowl and mix together until thoroughly combined, then beat in the butter. Sift together the flour and baking powder and fold into the butter mixture with the sugar. Mix until smooth but don't over mix, as this will result in denser muffins. Gently fold in the cranberries. Divide the mixture into the muffin cups—each should be about three-quarters full.

🥄 Mix together the topping ingredients and sprinkle over the muffins. Place in the preheated oven and bake 20 minutes or until firm to the touch. Remove from the oven, allow to cool in the pans 2–3 minutes, then turn out into a serving dish. These muffins are best eaten immediately or while still warm.

"English" Scones with Strawberry Preserve & Cream

Preparation time 12–15 minutes
Cooking time 7–10 minutes
Makes 10–12

2 cups (9 oz/250g) all-purpose flour
¼ teaspoon salt
4 teaspoons baking powder
3½ tablespoons (1¾ oz/50 g)
    butter, chilled and diced
⅔ cup (5 fl oz/150 ml) milk
a little water
milk or flour, to finish

To serve
strawberry preserve
whipped cream

❧ Preheat the oven to 450°F (230°C, Gas Mark 8). Sift the flour, salt, and baking powder into a bowl. Add the butter and rub in with the fingertips until the mixture resembles fine bread crumbs. Make a well in the center, pour in the milk, and mix to a soft dough. Add a little water if necessary.

❧ Turn the dough out onto a well-floured surface and knead quickly and lightly. Roll out the dough with a floured rolling pin or flatten with floured hands until it is ¾ inch (1.5 cm) thick. Cut into circles using a 2½-inch (6-cm) floured cookie cutter. Place the scones on a warmed cookie sheet.

❧ Shape the remaining dough into a ball, flatten into a circle, cut out more rounds, and place on the cookie sheet. Brush the scones with milk for a glazed finish or rub them with flour for a soft crust. Place in the preheated oven near the top 7–10 minutes until well risen and golden. Serve warm or cold with strawberry preserve and whipped cream.

Chocolate Party Cake

Preparation time 30 minutes
Cooking time 1 hour
Serves 14–16

14 oz (400 g) semisweet chocolate
1½ sticks (6 oz/175 g) unsalted
    butter, softened, plus extra
    for greasing
generous 1 cup (9 oz/250 g)
    light brown sugar
4 eggs
¾ cup (3½ oz/100 g) self-rising flour

½ cup (1¾ oz/50 g) unsweetened
    cocoa powder
1 cup (3½ oz/100 g) ground almonds
1¼ cups (10 fl oz/300 ml) heavy cream
generous 1 cup (9 oz/250 g)
    mascarpone cheese
1 tablespoon boiling water

✿ Preheat the oven to 325°F (160°C, Gas Mark 3) and grease and line the base and sides of an 8-inch (20-cm) round cake pan with parchment paper.

✿ Place 9 oz (250 g) of the chocolate and ⅓ cup (2½ fl oz/75 ml) water in a heatproof bowl and set over a saucepan of gently simmering water, making sure the bottom of the bowl doesn't touch the water. Heat, stirring occasionally, until the chocolate has melted and the mixture is thoroughly combined.

✿ Beat together the butter and sugar in a bowl until pale and creamy. Add the eggs one at a time, beating well between each addition. Stir in the melted chocolate, then sift the flour and cocoa into the bowl. Add the almonds and gently fold until thoroughly combined. Pour the mixture into the cake pan and level the surface. Place in the preheated oven and bake for about 1 hour or until risen and just firm to the touch. A metal skewer inserted into the center should come out slightly sticky. Remove the cake from the oven and cool in the pan on a cooling rack.

✿ When the cake is cold, cut it into 3 layers. Very lightly whip the cream, then sandwich the 3 layers together with the cream. Carefully transfer the cake to a serving plate.

🍫 Melt the remaining chocolate, as above. In a separate bowl, beat the mascarpone with 1 tablespoon boiling water. Add to the melted chocolate, mix well, and spread over the top and sides of the cake.

Rich Fruit Cake

Preparation time 45 minutes, plus cooling
Cooking time 3–3½ hours
Serves 16

1 cup (4½ oz/125 g) self-rising flour
scant 1⅔ cups (7 oz/200 g)
    all-purpose flour
¼ teaspoon salt
1 teaspoon ground allspice
½ teaspoon ground cinnamon
½ teaspoon ground nutmeg
2¼ sticks (9 oz/250 g) butter, plus
    extra for greasing
generous 1⅓ cups (9 oz/250 g) dark
    brown sugar
2 teaspoons molasses
5 eggs
scant ¼ cup (1¾ fl oz/50 ml)
    medium-dry sherry or strained
    cold tea

1½ teaspoons vanilla extract
1⅔ cups (9 oz/250 g) currants
1⅔ cups (9 oz/250 g) golden raisins
1⅔ cups (9 oz/250 g) prunes or
    dates, roughly chopped
1⅔ cups (9 oz/250 g) raisins
scant 1¾ cups (9 oz/250 g) candied
    citrus peel
generous 2½ cups (9 oz/250 g)
    ground almonds
1¼ cups (9 oz/250 g) candied
    cherries, halved
finely grated zest of 1 lemon
3–4 tablespoons brandy

♨ Preheat the oven to 275°F (140°C, Gas Mark 1) and grease and line the base and sides of a 9-inch (23-cm) round or 8-inch (20-cm) square baking pan with a double thickness of parchment paper. Line the outside with several thicknesses of brown kraft paper, standing at least 2 inches (5 cm) above the top of the pan.

♨ Sift the flours into a bowl with the salt, allspice, cinnamon, and nutmeg. In another large bowl, beat the butter with the sugar until light. Beat in the molasses. In a further bowl, lightly beat together the eggs, sherry or tea, and vanilla extract. Gradually beat half the egg mixture into the butter mixture, then fold in one-third of the sifted flours. Continue to add the egg and flour mixtures alternately, then mix in all the remaining ingredients except the brandy. Pour the batter into the pan and level the surface.

꙳ Place in the preheated oven and bake for 3–3¼ hours until a metal skewer inserted into the center comes out clean. Cover the cake with a double layer of parchment paper if the top starts to brown too much during cooking.

꙳ Remove the cake from the oven and let cool in the pan on a cooling rack before turning out onto the rack to cool completely. Prick all over with a fine skewer and spoon the brandy over the cake. Store in an airtight container and let mature for about 1 month before using.

Variation

꙳ For an Iced Fruit Cake, brush the cake all over with smooth apricot jelly, then cover with one recipe quantity marzipan (see page 82). Use half this quantity if you want to cover only the top of the cake. Ice the whole cake with 2–3 coats of thin royal icing (see page 83). Add further decorations made from ready-to-roll fondant and candy decorations, if liked.

Marzipan

Preparation time: 10 minutes
Makes enough to cover an 8-inch
(20-cm) square cake

generous 3 cups (10½ oz/300 g) ground
    almonds
1½ cups (10½ oz/300 g) superfine sugar,
    sifted
2 egg yolks
2 tablespoons lemon or orange juice
few drops of almond extract

❧ Mix the ground almonds and sugar in a bowl until thoroughly combined. Beat the egg yolks with the lemon or orange juice and stir into the dry ingredients. Work into a stiff paste and knead until smooth—the warmth of the hands brings out the oil in the ground almonds. If kneading makes the paste sticky, work in a little more sugar. If dry and crumbly, add a little more lemon or orange juice. If you are not using the marzipan immediately, wrap it in plastic wrap or foil and store in an airtight container for 2–3 days.

Royal Icing

Preparation time 25 minutes, plus standing
Makes 450 g (1 lb) icing

2 egg whites
¼ teaspoon lemon juice
4 cups (1 lb/450 g) confectioners' sugar, sifted
1 teaspoon glycerin

❧ Place the egg whites and lemon juice in a clean bowl. Using a clean wooden spoon, stir to break up the egg whites. Add enough confectioners' sugar to form the consistency of light cream, then continue mixing while adding small quantities of confectioners' sugar until it is all used up. Stir in the glycerin until well blended. Cover with damp plastic wrap, sealing well to exclude all air, then allow to stand before using so air bubbles can rise to the surface and burst. Stir thoroughly to disperse any air bubbles, then apply according to the recipe, using a metal spatula.

Bakers' notes

❧ Royal icing is the traditional icing used to cover celebration cakes. Depending on the consistency, it may be used for flat icing, peaked icing, or for piping on as decoration. As in this recipe, glycerin is often used in royal icing to help soften the icing, but should be used sparingly.

❧ Marzipan and royal icing contain raw egg, which should not be eaten by children, pregnant women, the elderly, or those recovering from serious illness, unless it is pasteurized. Look out for pasteurized eggs. If these are unavailable, then make up using dried egg whites.

Jottings & Tasting Notes

Use these pages to keep track of your favorite recipes from cookbooks, food magazines, and even websites. Simply fill in the recipe name along with the source, for example, the name of the cookbook and the relevant page number, plus any other notes you'd like to make.

Recipe

Source

Baking Notes

Recipe

Source

Baking Notes

Recipe

Source

Baking Notes

Recipe

Source

Baking Notes

Recipe

Source

Baking Notes

Recipe

Source

Baking Notes

Recipe

Source

Baking Notes

Recipe

Source

Baking Notes

Recipe

Source

Baking Notes

Recipe

Source

Makes/Serves

Testing & Tasting Notes

Ingredients

Method

Recipe

Source

Makes/Serves

Testing & Tasting Notes

Ingredients

Method

Recipe

Source

Makes/Serves

Testing & Tasting Notes

Ingredients

Method

"There are few hours in life more agreeable than the hour dedicated to the ceremony known as afternoon tea."

Henry James,
Portrait of a Lady

Recipe

Source

Makes/Serves

Testing & Tasting Notes

Ingredients

Method

Recipe
Source
Makes/Serves
Testing & Tasting Notes

Ingredients

Method

Recipe

Source

Makes/Serves

Testing & Tasting Notes

Ingredients

Method

Recipe

Source

Makes/Serves

Testing & Tasting Notes

Ingredients

Method

"I am not a glutton—
I am an explorer of food."

Erma Bombeck

Recipe

Source

Makes/Serves

Testing & Tasting Notes

Ingredients

Method

Recipe

Source

Makes/Serves

Testing & Tasting Notes

Ingredients

Method

*"Laughter is brightest
where food is best."*

Irish proverb

Recipe

Source

Makes/Serves

Testing & Tasting Notes

Ingredients

Method

COOKIES & TRAYBAKES

"Cookies are made of butter and love."

Norwegian proverb

Chocolate Chip Cookies

Preparation time 10 minutes
Cooking time 15–20 minutes
Makes 25

1⅛ sticks (4½ oz/125 g) butter, softened, plus
    extra for greasing
generous ¼ cup (1¾ oz/50 g) soft brown
    sugar
1 egg, beaten
1¼ cups (5¼ oz/150 g) self-rising flour
4½ oz (125 g) semisweet chocolate chips

✿ Preheat the oven to 350°F (180°C, Gas Mark 4) and lightly grease a cookie sheet. Put the butter and sugar in a bowl and beat together with a wooden spoon until light and fluffy. Beat in the egg and then sift in the flour. Add the chocolate chips and mix thoroughly.

✿ Put 25 teaspoonfuls of the mixture, slightly apart, on the cookie sheet and bake in the preheated oven 15–20 minutes until golden brown. Remove from the oven and leave on the cookie sheet 1 minute. Transfer to a cooling rack and let cool.

Variation

✿ For Oatmeal & Raisin Cookies, mix the butter and sugar as above. Add the egg and flour, replacing 2 tablespoons self-rising flour with 2 heaping tablespoons old-fashioned rolled oats. Add 1 teaspoon allspice to the flour. Omit the chocolate but add a scant cup (4½ oz/125 g) of raisins. Shape and cook the dough as above. These cookies are best eaten while they are still warm.

Flapjacks

Preparation time 10 minutes
Cooking time 35 minutes
Makes 16

7 tablespoons (3½ oz/100 g) butter or
    margarine, plus extra for greasing
3½ oz (100 g) vegetable shortening
scant ½ cup (3½ oz/100 g) turbinado sugar
4 tablespoons light corn syrup
3½ cups (12¼ oz/350 g) old-fashioned
    rolled oats

❧ Preheat the oven to 325°F (160°C, Gas Mark 3) and grease and line the base and sides of a 13 x 9 x 2-inch (33 x 23 x 5-cm) rectangular pan with parchment paper.

❧ Put the butter, vegetable fat, sugar, and light corn syrup in a saucepan over a low heat and heat gently, stirring continuously, until the butter and shortening are melted and the sugar has dissolved. Remove from the heat and stir in the oats until evenly coated.

❧ Transfer the mixture to the pan and spread out evenly. Bake in the preheated oven 35 minutes or until the mixture is a deep, golden brown. Remove from the oven and immediately score into 16 bars. Let cool in the pan and then cut into bars.

Linzer Cookies

Preparation time 35 minutes
Cooking time 16 minutes
Makes 16

⅓ cup (1¾ oz/50 g) hazelnuts
generous 1 cup (8 oz/225 g) all-purpose flour
⅓ cup (2¾ oz/75 g) superfine sugar
1⅜ tablespoons (5¼ oz/150 g) butter, diced
finely grated zest of ½ lemon
1 egg yolk
4 tablespoons seedless raspberry preserve
sifted confectioners' sugar, for dusting

❧ Preheat the oven to 350°F (180°C, Gas Mark 4). Grind the hazelnuts very finely in a coffee grinder or blender. Set aside. Put the flour and sugar in a bowl or a food processor. Add the butter and rub in with the fingertips or process until the mixture resembles fine bread crumbs. Stir in the ground hazelnuts and lemon zest, then mix in the egg yolk. Bring the mixture together with your hands to form a firm dough.

❧ Knead lightly on a lightly floured surface. Roll out half of the dough until ½ inch (1 cm) thick. Using a 2¼-inch (5.5-cm) fluted round cookie cutter, stamp out 16 circles and transfer to an ungreased cookie sheet. Using a 1-inch (2.5-cm) heart- or star-shaped cookie cutter, cut out shapes from the center of half the circles. Bake in the preheated oven 8 minutes or until pale golden. Leave the cookies to harden 1–2 minutes, then transfer to a cooling rack to cool. Meanwhile, repeat for the remaining dough.

❧ Divide the preserve evenly among the centers of the whole cookies and spread thickly, leaving a border of cookie showing. Cover with the hole-cut cookies, dust with a little sifted confectioners' sugar, and let cool completely before serving.

Chewy Nut
Chocolate Brownies

Preparation time 10 minutes,
**   plus cooling**
Cooking time 30 minutes
Makes 15

7 tablespoons (3½ oz/100 g) butter, plus extra
    for greasing
2¾ oz (75 g) semisweet chocolate
1 cup (7 oz/200 g) light brown sugar
2 eggs, beaten
few drops of vanilla extract
scant ½ cup (1¾ oz/50 g) ground almonds
2 tablespoons cornmeal
1¼ cups (5¼ oz/150 g) mixed nuts, toasted
    and roughly chopped
ice cream, to serve (optional)

🍴 Preheat the oven to 350°F (180°C, Gas Mark 4) and grease and line the base and sides of an 11 x 7-inch (28 x 18-cm) rectangular pan with parchment paper.

🍴 Place the butter and chocolate in a heatproof bowl and set over a saucepan of gently simmering water, making sure the bottom of the bowl does not touch the water. Heat, stirring occasionally, until the ingredients have melted. Mix to combine. Remove from the pan and stir in all the remaining ingredients until well combined.

🍴 Transfer the mixture into the pan and bake in the preheated oven 30 minutes or until slightly springy in the center. Remove from the oven and cool 10 minutes in the pan, then cut into 15 squares. Serve warm or cold with ice cream, if liked.

Chocolate Macaroons

Preparation time 10 minutes
Cooking time 15 minutes
Makes 25

2 egg whites
½ cup (3½ oz/100 g) superfine sugar
1⅓ cups (4½ oz/125 g) ground almonds
1¾ oz (50 g) bittersweet chocolate, grated
25 chocolate -covered coffee beans or
    chocolate chips, to decorate

🍮 Preheat the oven to 350°F (180°C, Gas Mark 4) and line a large cookie sheet with parchment paper. Beat the egg whites until stiff, then gradually beat in the sugar until the mixture is thick and glossy. Gently fold in the ground almonds and grated chocolate.

🍮 Put the mixture in a pastry bag fitted with a large plain decorating tip and pipe small rounds, about 1½ inches (4 cm) in diameter onto the cookie sheet. Alternatively, use a teaspoon.

🍮 Press a chocolate-covered coffee bean or chocolate chip into the center of each macaroon. Bake in the preheated oven 15 minutes or until slightly risen and just firm. Remove the cookies from the oven and cool on the cookie sheet.

Variations

🍮 For Plain Almond Macaroons, use 1⅓ cups (4½ oz/125 g) ground almonds, ¾ cup (5¼ oz/150 g) superfine sugar, 2 egg whites, and ½ teaspoon almond extract. Make as above.

🍮 For White Chocolate & Pistachio Macaroons, replace the bittersweet chocolate with 1¾ oz (50 g) white chocolate. Grind 1⅓ cups (4½ oz/125 g) pistachios in a coffee grinder or blender and use in place of the almonds. Make as above.

113

Plain Cookie Dough

Preparation time 50 minutes, plus chilling and cooling
Cooking time 15 minutes
Makes about 20 cookies

2 cups (9 oz/250 g) all-purpose
    flour, plus extra for dusting
2¼ sticks (9 oz/250 g) unsalted
    butter, chilled and diced, plus
    extra for greasing

1 cup (4½ oz/125 g) confectioners'
    sugar
2 egg yolks
2 teaspoons vanilla extract

☘ Preheat the oven to 350°F (180°C, Gas Mark 4) and lightly grease a cookie sheet. Place the flour in a bowl, add the butter, and rub in with the fingertips until the mixture resembles fine bread crumbs. Add the sugar, egg yolks, and vanilla extract and mix to a smooth dough. Wrap and chill for at least 30 minutes before using.

☘ Roll out the dough on a lightly floured surface and cut out using round or shaped cookie cutters, such as bunnies and ducks, as shown here. Space the dough shapes slightly apart on the cookie sheets, then reroll the trimmings to make extras. Bake in the preheated oven 10–15 minutes until pale golden. Remove from the oven and transfer to a cooling rack to cool.

Variation

☘ To decorate cookies first make the Glacé Icing. Place 1 egg white in a bowl, then gradually mix in 2 cups (9 oz/250 g) confectioners' sugar, sifted. Mix in 1 teaspoon lemon juice until smooth. Add extra water if the icing seems too thick. Divide the icing between two or more bowls, and color with liquid or paste food colorings, as liked. Set aside some white icing to pipe outlines and finishing features. Spoon the icing into pastry bags fitted with fine decorating tips, and pipe outlines around the edge of the cookies. Let harden 10 minutes. Fill in the rest of the surface of the cookie with the same color icing and let dry. Finally, pipe white icing outlines around the edge of the cookies and any finishing features.

Jottings & Tasting Notes

Use these pages to keep track of your favorite recipes from cookbooks, food magazines, and even websites. Simply fill in the recipe name along with the source, for example, the name of the cookbook and the relevant page number, plus any other notes you'd like to make.

Recipe

Source

Baking Notes

Recipe

Source

Baking Notes

Recipe

Source

Baking Notes

Recipe

Source

Baking Notes

Recipe

Source

Baking Notes

Recipe

Source

Baking Notes

Recipe

Source

Baking Notes

Recipe

Source

Baking Notes

Recipe

Source

Baking Notes

Recipe

Source

Makes/Serves

Testing & Tasting Notes

Ingredients

Method

Recipe

Source

Makes/Serves

Testing & Tasting Notes

Ingredients

Method

Recipe
Source
Makes/Serves
Testing & Tasting Notes

Ingredients

Method

Recipe

Source

Makes/Serves

Testing & Tasting Notes

Ingredients

Method

"All I really need is love, but a little chocolate now and then doesn't hurt."

Charles M. Schulz

Recipe
Source
Makes/Serves
Testing & Tasting Notes

Ingredients

Method

Recipe

Source

Makes/Serves

Testing & Tasting Notes

Ingredients

Method

Recipe

Source

Makes/Serves

Testing & Tasting Notes

Ingredients

Method

Recipe

Source

Makes/Serves

Testing & Tasting Notes

Ingredients

Method

"Tell me what you eat,
I'll tell you who you are."

Anthelme Brillat-Savarin

Recipe

Source

Makes/Serves

Testing & Tasting Notes

Ingredients

Method

Recipe

Source

Makes/Serves

Testing & Tasting Notes

Ingredients

Method

DESSERTS

*"Life is uncertain.
Eat dessert first."*

Ernestine Ulmer

Sticky Toffee Pudding

Preparation time 20 minutes
Cooking time 45–50 minutes
Serves 8

¾ cup (4½ oz/125 g) chopped
　　pitted dried dates
1 stick (4 oz/115 g) unsalted
　　butter, softened, plus extra
　　for greasing
½ cup (3½ oz/100 g) superfine
　　sugar
2 teaspoons vanilla bean paste
3 eggs
scant 1½ cups (6 oz/175 g) self-
　　rising flour

1 teaspoon baking powder
heavy cream, to serve

Sauce
1¼ cups (10 fl oz/300 ml) heavy
　　cream
¾ cup (5¼ oz/150 g) light brown
　　sugar
4 tablespoons (2 oz/60 g) butter

🍤 Put the dates in a small saucepan with ⅔ cup (5 fl oz/150 ml) water and bring to a boil. Simmer gently 5 minutes or until the dates are soft. Blend to a puree using a food processor. Let cool.

🍤 Put half the cream in a heavy-bottomed saucepan with the brown sugar and butter and heat, stirring occasionally, until the sugar dissolves. Bring to a boil and simmer gently about 5 minutes or until the sauce turns to a rich, dark caramel. Stir in the remaining cream and set aside.

🍤 Preheat the oven to 350°F (180°C, Gas Mark 4) and grease and base line eight metal ⅔-cup (5-fl-oz/150-ml) pudding molds with circles of parchment paper. Put the butter, sugar, vanilla bean paste, eggs, flour, and baking powder in a bowl and beat until pale and creamy. Stir in the date puree and divide into the pudding molds. Place the molds in a roasting pan, pour boiling water into the pan to a depth of ¾ inch (2 cm), and cover with foil. Bake in the preheated oven 35–40 minutes until they are risen and firm to the touch.

🍤 Reheat the toffee sauce. Loosen the edges of the molds and invert onto serving plates. Cover with sauce and serve with heavy cream.

Rich Vanilla Custard

Preparation time 10 minutes,
plus infusing
Cooking time 10–15 minutes
Serves 6

1 vanilla bean, split lengthwise
1¼ cups (10 fl oz/300 ml) whole milk
1¼ cups (10 fl oz/300 ml) light cream
6 egg yolks
2 tablespoons superfine sugar

❧ Put the split vanilla bean, milk, and cream in a saucepan over medium-low heat and bring almost to a boil. Remove from the heat and set aside to infuse 15 minutes. Meanwhile, beat together the egg yolks and sugar in a bowl with a balloon whisk until thick and pale. Lift the vanilla bean out of the milk mixture and scrape the black seeds into the pan. Discard the bean pod.

❧ Pour the milk mixture over the creamed eggs and sugar, beating well. Pour the mixture into a clean pan and cook over medium heat, stirring constantly with a wooden spoon, until the custard thickly coats the back of the spoon. This will take about 5–10 minutes. Don't be tempted to raise the heat or the custard might curdle. Serve warm.

Variations

❧ For Chocolate Custard, omit the vanilla and stir 2 oz (50 g) chopped bittersweet chocolate into the sauce as soon as it has thickened, stirring until melted.

❧ For Coffee Custard, omit the vanilla and add 1 tablespoon instant espresso powder when heating the milk.

Bread & Butter Pudding with Pecans

Preparation time 10 minutes, plus chilling
Cooking time 30–35 minutes
Serves 4–6

14 oz (400 g) day-old bread
½ cup (1¾ oz/50 g) pecan nuts,
    broken into pieces
1⅔ cups (14 fl oz/400 ml) whole milk
3 eggs
⅓ cup (2½ oz/75 g) superfine sugar
1 teaspoon vanilla extract

1 teaspoon ground cinnamon
2 tablespoons (1 oz/25 g) butter

To serve
confectioners' sugar, for dusting
maple syrup
light cream (optional)

❧ Cut the bread into 1-inch (2.5-cm) cubes, leaving the crust on. Place in a buttered 6-cup (50-fl-oz/1.5-l) shallow rectangular baking dish and sprinkle with the pecans.

❧ Lightly beat the milk, eggs, sugar, vanilla, and cinnamon together in a bowl, then strain over the bread so that it is coated in the milk mixture, pressing any remains through the strainer with the back of a spoon. Dot the top with the butter, cover with foil, and chill overnight in the refrigerator.

❧ When ready to serve, remove the foil from the dish and bake in a preheated oven at 350°F (180°C, Gas Mark 4) 30–35 minutes until the top is golden and crispy and the custard is set. Check after 20–25 minutes and cover with foil if the bread seems to be overbrowning.

❧ Dust with confectioners' sugar and let stand for 10 minutes. Cut into large squares and transfer to serving plates. Serve warm, drizzled with maple syrup and cream, if liked.

Vanilla Bean Crème Brûlée

**Preparation time: 20 minutes,
plus infusing and chilling
Cooking time: 25–30 minutes
Serves 6**

1 vanilla bean, split lengthwise, or 1 teaspoon
    vanilla extract
2½ cups (20 fl oz/600 ml) heavy cream
8 egg yolks
4 tablespoons superfine sugar
3 tablespoons confectioners' sugar

🥄 Put the split vanilla bean and cream in a saucepan over medium-low heat and bring almost to a boil. Remove from the heat and set aside to infuse 15 minutes. Lift the vanilla bean out of the cream and scrape the black seeds into the pan. Discard the bean pod. If using vanilla extract, heat the milk to almost boiling, remove from the heat, and add the extract—there is no need to infuse. Meanwhile preheat the oven to 350°F (180°C, Gas Mark 4).

🥄 Use a fork to mix together the eggs and sugar in a bowl. Reheat the cream and then gradually mix into the eggs and sugar. Strain the custard into six ⅔-cup (5-fl-oz/150-ml) custard cups or ramekins.

🥄 Place the custard cups in a roasting pan and pour boiling water into the pan to come halfway up their sides. Bake in the preheated oven 20–25 minutes until the brûlées are just set with a slight softness to the touch. Leave the dishes to cool in the water, then lift them out and chill 3–4 hours.

🥄 About 25 minutes before serving, sprinkle the tops with the confectioners' sugar. Caramelize under the broiler and then leave at room temperature until served.

Lemon Meringue Pie

Preparation time 40 minutes,
    plus chilling and standing
Cooking time 35–40 minutes
Serves 6

13¼ oz (375 g) premade or sweet
    shortcrust pastry (see page 42)
a little flour, for dusting
1 cup (7 oz/200 g) superfine sugar
⅓ cup (1½ oz/40 g) cornstarch
grated zest and juice of 2 lemons

4 eggs, separated
about 1 cup (8 fl oz/240 ml) water

✎ Roll out the pastry on a lightly floured surface until it is large enough to line an 8-inch (20-cm) deep-dish, loose-bottomed pie pan. Line the pan with the pastry. Trim off the excess around the rim, prick the base, and chill 15 minutes. Meanwhile preheat the oven to 375°F (190°C, Gas Mark 5).

✎ Line the pastry with parchment paper, add pie weights or macaroni, and blind bake in the preheated oven 15 minutes. Remove the paper and weights and bake a further 5 minutes.

✎ Put ⅓ cup (2¾ oz/75 g) of the sugar in a bowl with the cornstarch and lemon zest. Add the egg yolks and mix until smooth. Make the lemon juice up to 1¼ cups (10 fl oz/300 ml) with water, pour into a saucepan and bring to a boil. Gradually mix into the yolk mixture, beating until smooth. Pour the mixture back into the pan and bring to a boil, beating until very thick. Pour into the baked shell and level the surface.

✎ Beat the egg whites until they form stiff peaks. Gradually beat in the remaining sugar, then beat 1–2 minutes more until very thick and glossy. Spoon over the lemon layer to cover completely and swirl with a spoon. Reduce the oven to 350°F (180°C, Gas Mark 4) and cook 15–20 minutes until the meringue is cooked through. Remove from the oven and let stand at least 15 minutes before serving. Serve warm or cold.

Variation

✿ For Citrus Meringue Pie, mix the grated zest of 1 lime, 1 lemon, and ½ small orange with the cornstarch. Squeeze the juice from the fruits and make up the volume to 1¼ cups (10 fl oz/300 ml) with water. Make as above.

Florentine Vanilla Cheesecake

Preparation time 25 minutes,
  plus chilling
Cooking time 45 minutes
Serves 8–10

4 oz (125 g) bittersweet chocolate
scant ½ cup (2 oz/50 g) slivered
  almonds, lightly toasted
2½ tablespoons candied citrus peel,
  finely chopped
6 candied cherries, finely chopped
6 oz (175 g) graham crackers,
  crushed
4 tablespoons (2 oz/60 g) butter,
  melted, plus extra for greasing

17 oz (480 g) cream cheese
1 teaspoon vanilla extract
1⅔ cup (5 fl oz/150 ml)
  heavy cream
⅔ cup (5 oz/150 g)
  Greek-style yogurt
generous ½ cup (4 oz/125 g)
  superfine sugar
3 eggs

🍮 Preheat the oven to 325°F (160°C, Gas Mark 3). Grease an 8-inch
(20-cm) loose-bottomed cake pan and line the sides with a strip of
parchment paper. Chop half the chocolate into small pieces. Lightly
crush the almonds and mix in a bowl with the chocolate, candied fruits,
graham crackers, and butter until thoroughly combined. Turn the crumb
mixture into the pan and push it firmly into the bottom and slightly up
the sides to form a shell.

🍮 Beat the cream cheese and vanilla extract in a bowl until smooth.
Beat in the cream, yogurt, sugar, and eggs to make a smooth batter, then
pour into the cookie case. Bake in the preheated oven 45 minutes or until
the surface feels just firm to the touch around the edges but is still wobbly
in the center. Turn off the heat and let the cheesecake cool in the oven.
Transfer to the fridge and chill well.

🍮 Transfer to a serving plate and peel away the lining paper. Melt
the remaining chocolate in a small bowl set over a pan of gently
simmering water, then drizzle it around the top edges of the cheesecake.
Chill until ready to serve.

Berry Crisp

**Preparation time 10 minutes
Cooking time 30 minutes
Serves 4**

2½ cups (10 oz/300 g) cranberries
1 cup (5 oz/150 g) blackberries
generous 1 cup (5 oz/150 g) blueberries
⅓ cup (3 oz/75 g) superfine sugar
Rich vanilla custard (see page 141) or vanilla
      ice cream, to serve

Topping
1½ cups (2¾ oz/75 g) fresh bread crumbs
¾ cup (2¾ oz/75 g) ground almonds
5 tablespoons (2¾ oz/75 g) butter,
      softened and diced
4 tablespoons superfine sugar
¼ cup (1 oz/25 g) slivered almonds

❧ Preheat the oven to 350°F (180°C, Gas Mark 4). Put the fruits into a saucepan with 4 tablespoons water, cover, and cook over a gentle heat for 10 minutes or until just tender. Stir in the sugar and then tip the fruit mixture into a shallow ovenproof baking dish, leaving room for the topping.

❧ To make the topping, put the bread crumbs, ground almonds, butter, and sugar into a bowl and rub the butter in with the fingertips until the mixture resembles fine crumbs. Sprinkle the topping over the top of the fruit, then sprinkle over the slivered almonds. Bake in the preheated oven 20–25 minutes until crisp and golden. Cover with foil after 15 minutes if overbrowning.

❧ Delicious served with rich vanilla custard or scoops of vanilla ice cream.

Mini Pavlovas with Mixed Fresh Berries

Preparation time 5 minutes
Cooking time 20 minutes
Makes 15–18

3 egg whites
generous ¾ cup (6 oz/175 g)
    superfine sugar

Topping
1¼ cups (10 fl oz/300 ml) heavy
    cream, whipped
about 15 oz (425 g) mixed berries
    such as strawberries,
    blueberries, & raspberries

❧ Preheat the oven to 300°F (150°C, Gas Mark 2) and line a cookie sheet with parchment paper. Place the egg whites in a clean and dry large bowl. Make sure there is no egg yolk in the egg whites, as the tiniest amount of egg yolk will prevent the whites from beating. Scoop out with a piece of shell if there is. Beat the egg whites until they form very stiff, moist-looking peaks. Gradually beat in the remaining sugar a teaspoonful at a time, then beat 1–2 minutes more until very thick and glossy.

❧ Spoon the meringue into mounds on the cookie sheet and shape into circles. Use the back of the spoon to make swirls in the meringue and small peaks. Place in the preheated oven, turn the oven temperature down to 275°F (140°C, Gas Mark 2), and bake 20 minutes or until the meringues are crisp and easily lift off the paper. If they stick to the paper, bake 5 minutes more and test again. Turn the oven off and leave in the oven to cool completely. Spread with the whipped heavy cream and top with the berries. Refrigerate until served.

Variations

❧ For Meringue Cookies, spoon the above mixture onto the lined cookie sheet to make 15–18 meringues, leaving about 2 inches (5 cm) between them. Bake in the preheated oven 20 minutes or until the meringues are crisp and easily lift off the paper (as above). To make

colored meringue, after you've added the sugar, beat in liquid or paste food coloring, a little at a time, until the desired color is reached.

❧ For Hazelnut Meringues, beat 4 egg whites until they form soft peaks, then slowly add generous 1 cup (8oz/225g) superfine sugar until very stiff and shiny. Fold in ½ teaspoon white wine vinegar and ¼ teaspoon vanilla extract followed by 1⅓ cups (3½ oz/100 g) ground hazelnuts. Spoon the mixture onto the lined cookie sheet to make 25 mini meringues. Bake in a preheated oven, 225°F (110°C, Gas Mark ¼), 45–60 minutes until the meringues are firm and easily peel off the paper. Remove from the oven and cool on a cooling rack. Decorate with scant ½ cup (3½ oz/100 g) crème fraîche and generous 1½ cups (6 oz/ 175 g) red currants, left as sprigs.

Jottings & Tasting Notes

Use these pages to keep track of your favorite recipes from cookbooks, food magazines, and even websites. Simply fill in the recipe name along with the source, for example, the name of the cookbook and the relevant page number, plus any other notes you'd like to make.

Recipe

Source
Baking Notes

Recipe

Source
Baking Notes

Recipe

Source
Baking Notes

Recipe

Source
Baking Notes

Recipe

Source

Baking Notes

Recipe

Source

Baking Notes

Recipe

Source

Baking Notes

Recipe

Source

Baking Notes

Recipe

Source

Baking Notes

Recipe

Source

Makes/serves

Testing and Tasting Notes

Ingredients

Method

*"Stressed spelt backwards
is desserts."*

Barbara Enberg

Recipe
Source
Makes/Serves
Testing & Tasting Notes

Ingredients

Method

Recipe
Source
Makes/Serves
Testing & Tasting Notes

Ingredients

Method

Recipe
Source

Makes/Serves

Testing & Tasting Notes

Ingredients

Method

Recipe

Source

Makes/Serves

Testing & Tasting Notes

Ingredients

Method

"Pray sir, take away this pudding. It has no theme."

Winston Churchill

Recipe

Source

Makes/Serves

Testing & Tasting Notes

Ingredients

Method

Recipe

Source

Makes/Serves

Testing & Tasting Notes

Ingredients

Method

Recipe

Source

Makes/Serves

Testing & Tasting Notes

Ingredients

Method

Recipe

Source

Makes/Serves

Testing & Tasting Notes

Ingredients

Method

Recipe

Source

Makes/Serves

Testing & Tasting Notes

Ingredients

Method

Recipe

Source

Makes/Serves

Testing & Tasting Notes

Ingredients

Method

Recipe

Source

Makes/Serves

Testing & Tasting Notes

Ingredients

Method

Acknowledgments

Getty Images/Johanna Doorenbosch 149; /Dorling Kindersley 141.

Octopus Publishing Group/Stephen Conroy 6, 8, 42, 43, 79, 115; /Ian Garlick 12, 17, 70, /Will Heap 47, 145; /Jeremy Hopley 143; /William Lingwood 108; /David Munns 5, 72, 73; /Emma Neish 74, 112; /Lis Parsons 7, 11, 81, 82, 111; /William Shaw 16, 138, 147; /Ian Wallace 40, 106, 113; /Philip Webb 76.

Thinkstock/Hemera 109; /iStockphoto 83.

Publisher: Sarah Ford
Managing Editor: Clare Churly
Consultant Editor: Camilla Davis
Designer: Eoghan O'Brien
Layout Designer: Clare Barber
Picture Librarian: Jennifer Veall
Production Manager: Katherine Hockley